EPP
9
I0605381
9
8A

SURVIVOR: FORGED BY FIRE

WORDS BY JEFF PROBST

PHOTOS CURATED BY SCOTT DUNCAN

Simon & Schuster
New York Amsterdam/Antwerp London Toronto Sydney/Melbourne New Delhi

SURVIVOR ISN'T JUST A GAME.
IT'S A JOURNEY. ONE THAT CALLS TO THE ADVENTURER INSIDE US ALL.

In the summer of 2000, a bold British television producer named Mark Burnett brought *Survivor* to American audiences, and with it, a new kind of storytelling. What he launched was more than a show. It was the start of one of the greatest adventures ever told.

For 25 years and 50 seasons, players from every walk of life have answered that call, leaving behind the comforts of home to test themselves against the jungles, the elements, and one another.

Forged by Fire invites you inside this extraordinary odyssey through never-before-seen cinematic images that capture the heart of the player, the spirit of the crew, and the spark that has kept this adventure burning for 50 unforgettable seasons.

Alongside these images, I share personal reflections—sparked by a photo or a stage of the game—and a few of my handwritten production diary entries from the show's early days.

Together, they reveal the resilience and extraordinary potential *Survivor* brings out in its players . . . and in all of us.

Their adventure . . . and ours . . . begins the moment they say "yes."

Step inside.

The fire is waiting.

—Jeff

This photo triggers an instant sense memory for me. It was taken on the morning of day one of our first season, just hours before we would abandon the players and begin the game.

It's wild how a single image can unlock so much—how vividly it brings me back.

It's crazy that even after 25 years, I can still feel it, as if it just happened.

Standing there...knowing, somehow, that *Survivor* was going to change my life. I just didn't know how.

I took it all seriously right from the start. After I got the job, but in the weeks before I left for Pulau Tiga, I decided to go to therapy—not for myself, but to try to get a better understanding of what the players were about to encounter. What happens to a person when you take away everything familiar? When you drop them into the middle of a jungle and leave them to figure it out?

I crammed in as many sessions as I could, trying to imagine the emotional shifts, the moments of doubt, the ways they might surface—sometimes in ways even the players themselves wouldn't see coming.

I also studied group dynamics, and I dove deep into Joseph Campbell, searching for the threads of *Survivor* inside the hero's journey.

I kept a folder filled with all my notes, little reminders about the ways groups could influence individual thinking, and how difficult and important trust would be, given the players are strangers.

I just wanted to be of service to the format, whatever that ended up meaning.

What I didn't realize at the time was that I wasn't just stepping into a job—I was stepping into a new life. I had my own threshold guardians to face, my own obstacles to overcome. And if you'd asked me back then what I was searching for...I wouldn't have had an answer.

I was just stepping into the unknown.

But even then, something inside me liked the feeling of not knowing. I've come to learn there's something powerful about that discomfort—it means you're standing at the edge of something important, even if it's not always enjoyable at the time.

And now, looking at this photo 25 years later, what strikes me most is the realization that the journey isn't over.

I'm still in it.

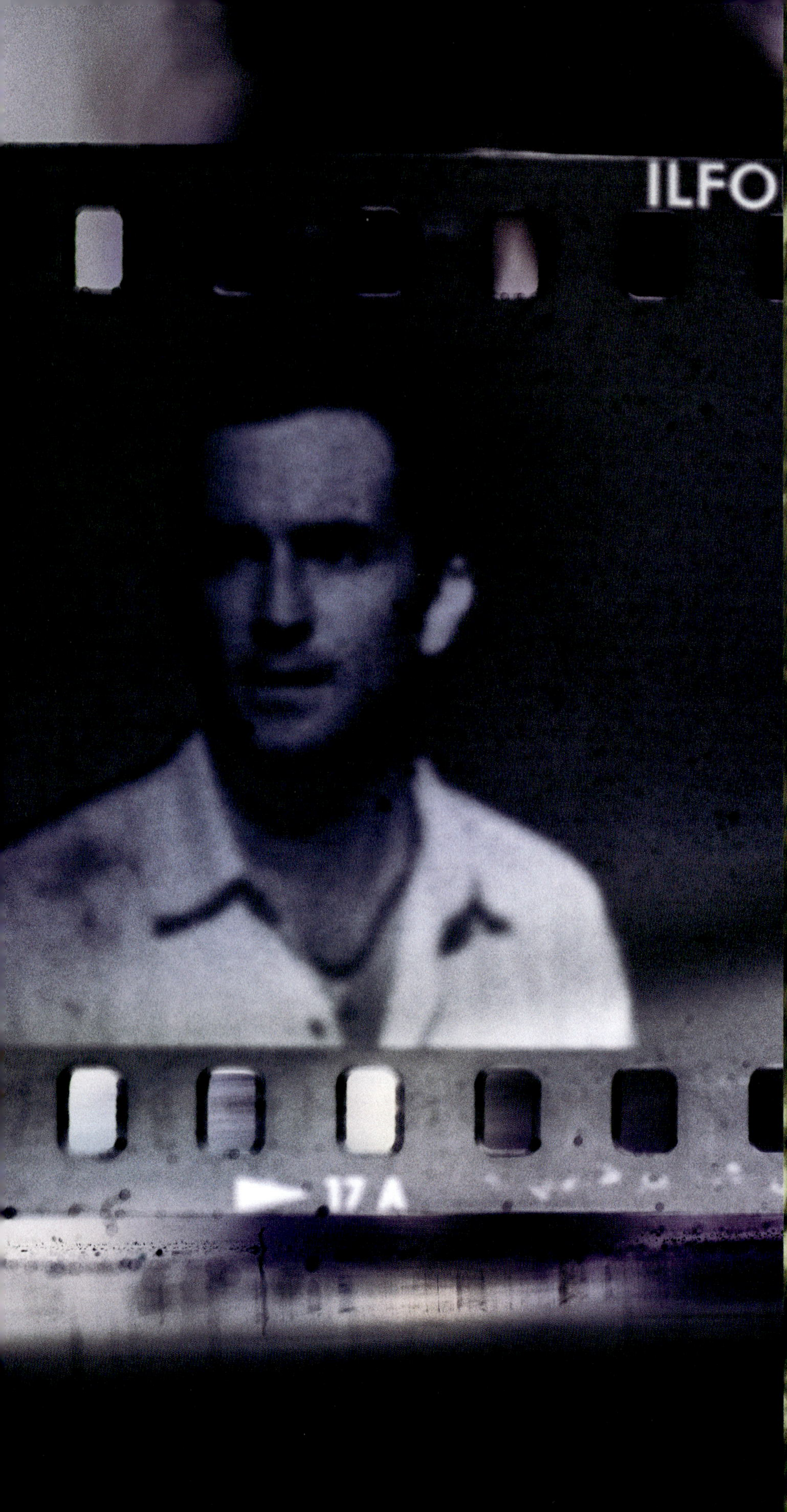

ILFO

17 A

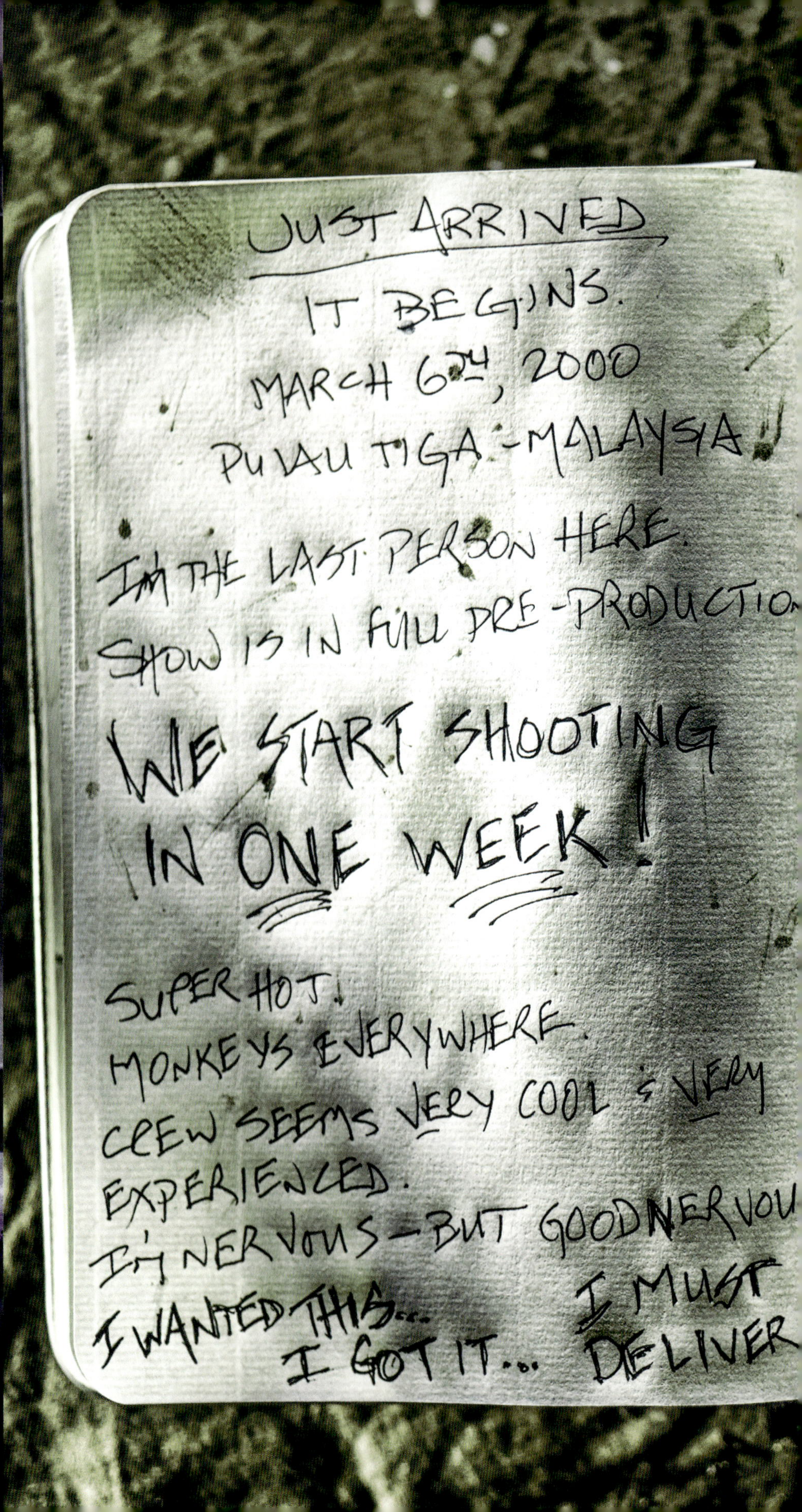

JUST ARRIVED

IT BEGINS.

MARCH 6TH, 2000

PULAU TIGA - MALAYSIA!!

I'M THE LAST PERSON HERE.

SHOW IS IN FULL PRE-PRODUCTION

WE START SHOOTING IN ONE WEEK!

SUPER HOT!

MONKEYS EVERYWHERE.

CREW SEEMS VERY COOL & VERY EXPERIENCED.

I'M NERVOUS - BUT GOOD NERVOU

I WANTED THIS... I GOT IT... I MUST DELIVER

ALKED WITH MARK FOR TWO
HOURS — HE IS VERY **CLEAR** —

THIS IS AN
UNSCRIPTED...
LIVE...
SPONTANEOUS...
EXPERIENCE.

E WILL HAVE TO REACT
TO WHAT IS HAPPENING...
AS IT HAPPENS...
IN REAL TIME.

GIANT MONITOR
LIZARD IN MY
ROOM.

THE ARRIVAL

The real adventure begins the moment a player says yes, leaving their ordinary world behind to embark on a journey into the unknown.

They don't realize it yet, but the journey is already changing them—forever altering how they see themselves . . . and how the world sees them.

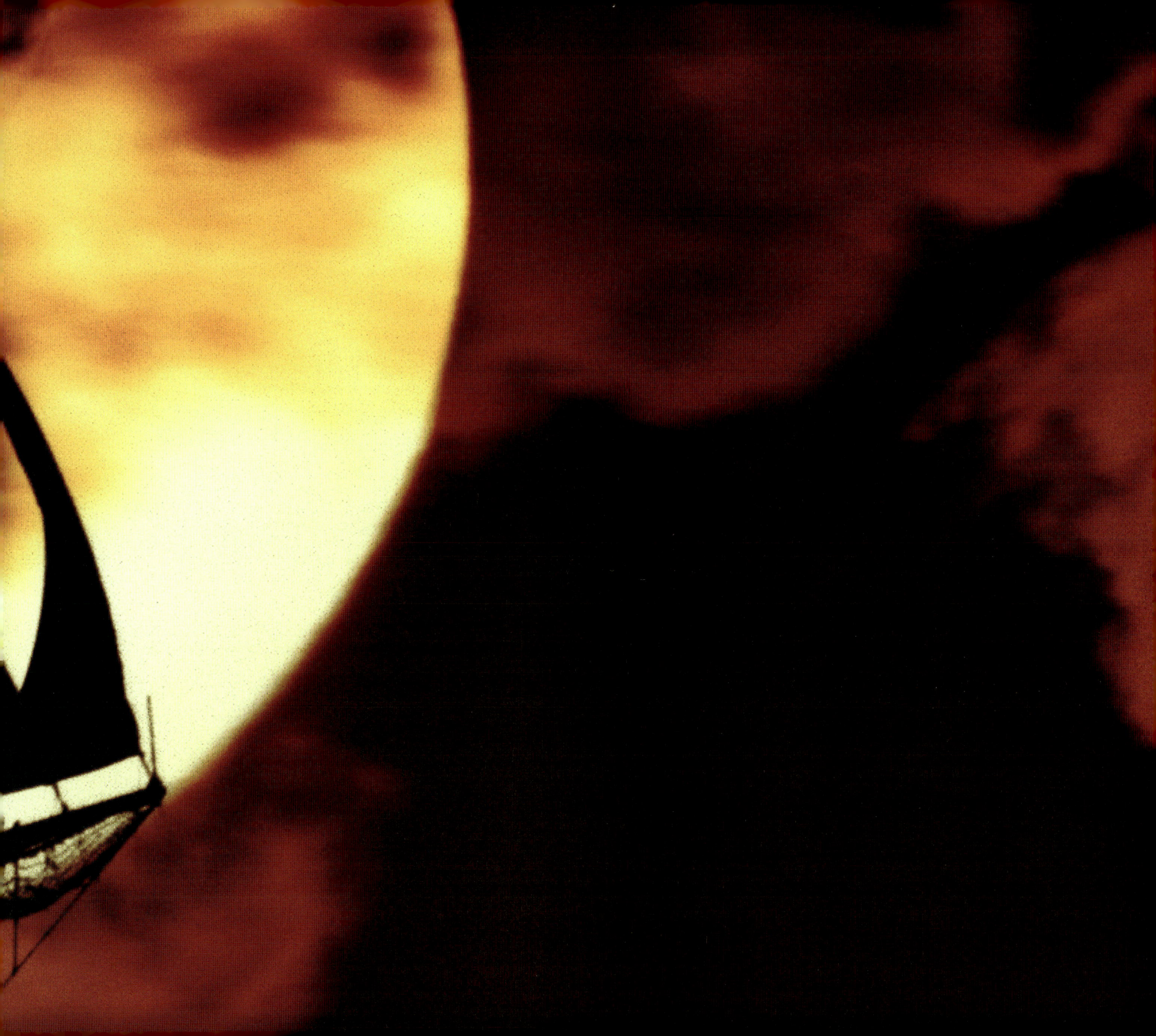

One of my favorite moments of any season is when we give the players their buffs. Because in that very brief period of time, I can see so much in their eyes—excitement, fear, joy, nerves—and because I know what's coming.

The buff signifies that a player has left behind their familiar world...and stepped into ours.

From this point forward, that small piece of stretchy fabric will bear witness to every high and every heartbreak. It'll ride shotgun through the storms, the hunger, the blindsides, the victories.

Their buff becomes their uniform, their identity. They'll wear it on their head, around their neck, over their face. They'll sweat into it. Cry into it. And if things go well, they'll bleed into it.

And by the time their journey is over, their buff will be sun-faded, salt-stained, and fully transformed—just like them.

A player's buff is their most sacred and cherished *Survivor* possession.

Because the buff is proof.

DAVID vs GOLIATH
OUTLAST

SURVIVOR
50
THE HANDS OF THE FANS

TREE MAIL

THE JUNGLE

The jungle offers no welcome.
It surrounds them. Alive, watching, indifferent.

Every step forward is a negotiation.
Every moment, a test.
This is where the adventure reveals its teeth.

Stripped of certainty, tested by the elements, doubt creeps in . . .
Each of them haunted by a single question . . . "Can I do this?"

INSECT
REPELLENT

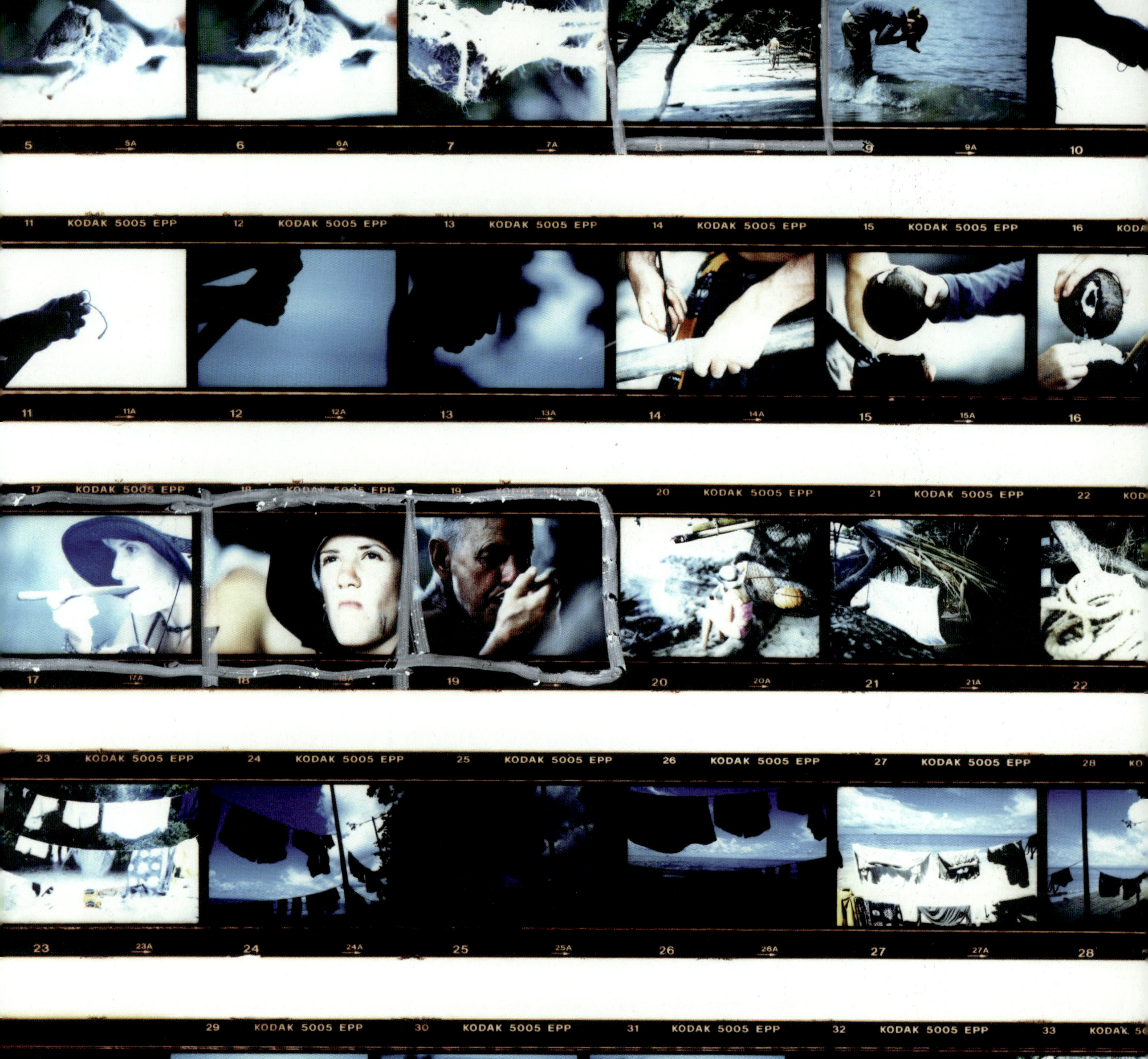

5 5A 6 6A 7 7A 8 8A 9 9A 10
11 KODAK 5005 EPP 12 KODAK 5005 EPP 13 KODAK 5005 EPP 14 KODAK 5005 EPP 15 KODAK 5005 EPP 16
11 11A 12 12A 13 13A 14 14A 15 15A 16
17 KODAK 5005 EPP 18 KODAK 5005 EPP 19 20 KODAK 5005 EPP 21 KODAK 5005 EPP 22
17 17A 18 18A 19 20 20A 21 21A 22
23 KODAK 5005 EPP 24 KODAK 5005 EPP 25 KODAK 5005 EPP 26 KODAK 5005 EPP 27 KODAK 5005 EPP 28
23 23A 24 24A 25 25A 26 26A 27 27A 28
29 KODAK 5005 EPP 30 KODAK 5005 EPP 31 KODAK 5005 EPP 32 KODAK 5005 EPP 33

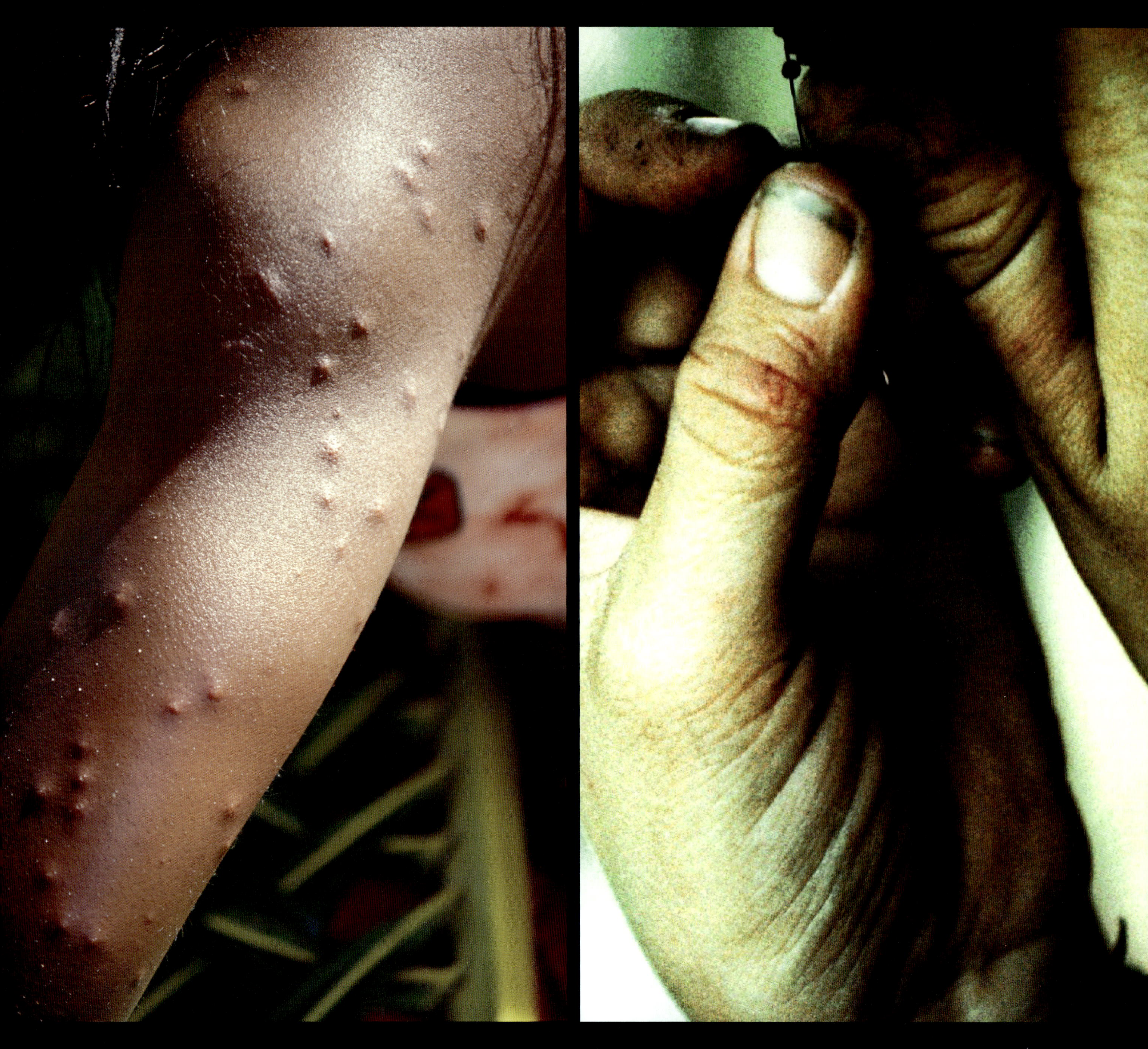

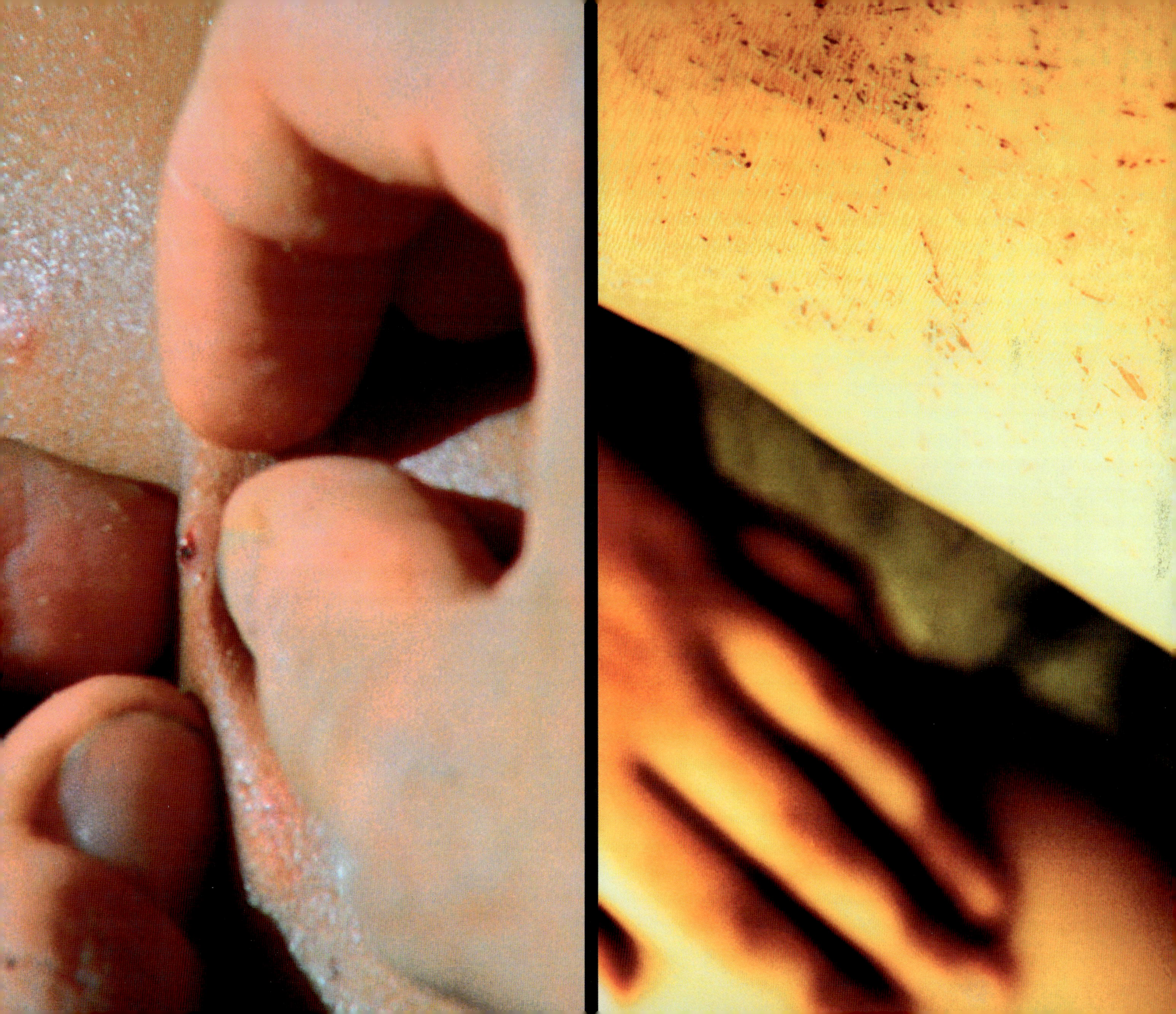

2 KODAK E200 3 KODAK E200 4 KODAK E200 5 KODAK E200 6 KODAK E200 7 KOD 2 KODAK E200 3 KODAK E200 4

KODAK E200

KODAK 5005 EPP

KODAK 5005 EPP

THE HANDS

SURVIVOR: ALL STARS
DAY 9 (NOV 11 2003) U.S.
TWO HOURS AFTER TRIBAL.
I JUST HEARD THE LOUDEST
CRACK OF THUNDER I HAVE
EVER HEARD IN MY LIFE.
ALL PHONES ARE OUT. INTERNET
DEAD. DEAD. IT'S UNREAL.
FIRST TIME IN EIGHT SEASONS I
AM WORRIED ABOUT THE PLAYERS.
EVERYBODY ON RADIOS CHECKING
WITH THE BEACHES—PLAYERS OK!
NO WORDS. JUST LISTENING. IT'S
POUNDING. THEY ARE DEFINITELY
EARNING THE TITLE OF:
ALL STARS!
BOOM!
3AM. ANOTHER
CRACK. NEARLY
BLEW MY WINDOW
OUT. LIT UP THE
ENTIRE PACIFIC!
OCEAN.
THIS IS INSANE!
DAY 12 — TRIBAL NOV. 14, 2003
BIG DISCUSSION ABOUT ROB
+ AMBER. THEY SEEM TO BE
A COUPLE.

54
KODAK EPP 6005

DATE:
TIME OF DAY: 0845
OPERATOR: DEAN
TAPE: D-A
-Robb + Amber cut
- Jenna +
chuck
peels

THE ARENA

It is here where players test themselves—not just against others,
but against their own limits.

These battles require more than strength.
They demand resolve, clarity, and the courage to be seen.

Pain and triumph walk side by side.
This is where one moment can shift everything,
as you rise in the eyes of your tribe or fall beneath the weight of it all.

Some emerge forged.
Others fall to pieces.
But no one walks away untouched.

BU
GONDOL
SURVIVOR
GONDOL

OUTWIT
OUTPLAY
OUTLAST
45
SURVIVOR

OUT

Anytime someone mentions the final-three immunity challenge in *Survivor: Palau* (Ba-Ba-Booey), it's always about how long it lasted . . . 12 hours—the longest immunity challenge in *Survivor* history. Two men bobbing in the water, refusing to give in to the intense pain . . . a pure test of will.

But what strikes me today, years later, is what I didn't see at the time.

When we tested the challenge with our Dream Team, it lasted about an hour, so we assumed a similar result with the players. But five hours in, only Katie had dropped, and Ian and Tom were still locked in.

The sun began to set. We had no lights. We floated in torches to light their faces, but Tom objected. He pointed out we'd never said anything about smoke in the rules. He was absolutely right. So as we scrambled to get lights and generators from basecamp, Tom and Ian continued to battle. At one point, rain rolled in, soaking everything. Then the sun returned with punishing heat. Still, neither man moved.

For nearly 12 hours I watched from my dock—sitting, standing, lying down—and I remember the creeping panic as it became clear: Neither was backing down.

It is only after 25 years of reflection that I now see what was really happening. This showdown was not about pain tolerance. It was an examination of motivation.

Tom and Ian both wanted something. But they didn't want the same thing. And that's what makes this challenge so truly memorable.

Tom wanted to win—both this challenge and the entire game. That was his singular, powerful drive. Ian had an equally powerful drive but his was very different. Ian was younger and emotionally torn up over how he'd played. He had hurt people. Betrayed their trust. He wasn't wrestling with endurance. He was wrestling with guilt.

And then came the moment when the two motives fully confronted each other.

Tom made an offer. He said, "Ian, if you let me win, I'll take you to the end with me."

If Ian could trust Tom's word, it was a pretty good offer, ensuring Ian would have a spot at the final Tribal Council and a shot at the million. But for Ian, it wasn't about winning the game. It was about winning back his integrity.

Ian replied: "I'm not doing this on your terms, Tom."

And a short while later, Ian made a counteroffer—his terms.

He said, "I'll drop out, Tom, but only if you don't take me and take Katie instead. Because that's the only way I can win back your respect. And hers. And that's more important to me than winning this game."

That was the most important turning point of the entire challenge. Tom paused for a moment, mostly for dramatic effect, and then said, "If that's what you want, then that's what I'll do."

And that was it. Ian stepped down.

In that moment, both players got what they came for.

Tom got what he wanted. He went on to win the season.

Ian got what he needed. He repaired two relationships that mattered more to him than the million dollars.

It's a beautiful example of what *Survivor* can offer when everything lines up just right. On the surface it's remembered as the longest immunity challenge in *Survivor* history. But when you strip away everything—the duration, the production scramble, the chaos of the moment—what you're left with is a quiet, human negotiation under extreme pressure. A battle of two individual motives, slowly revealed, then resolved.

Elapsed Time:
2 Hours 3 Minutes
Elapsed Time:
3 Hours 18 Minutes
Elapsed Time:
4 Hours
Elapsed Time:
4 Hours 51 Minutes

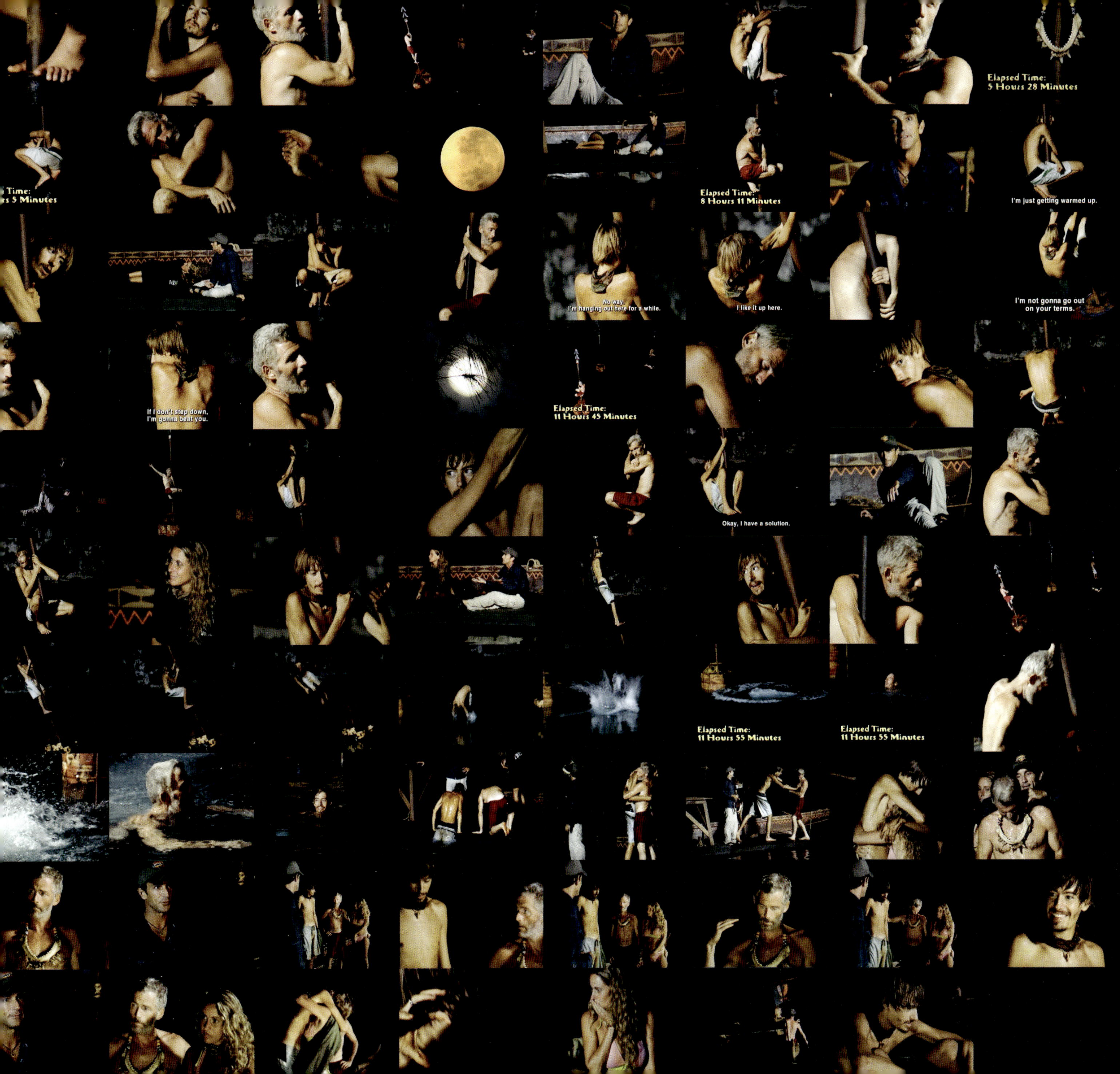
Elapsed Time:
5 Hours 28 Minutes
Elapsed Time:
8 Hours 11 Minutes
I'm just getting warmed up.
No way.
I'm hanging out here for a while.
I like it up here.
I'm not gonna go out
on your terms.
If I don't step down,
I'm gonna beat you.
Elapsed Time:
11 Hours 45 Minutes
Okay, I have a solution.
Elapsed Time:
11 Hours 55 Minutes
Elapsed Time:
11 Hours 55 Minutes

SURVIVOR

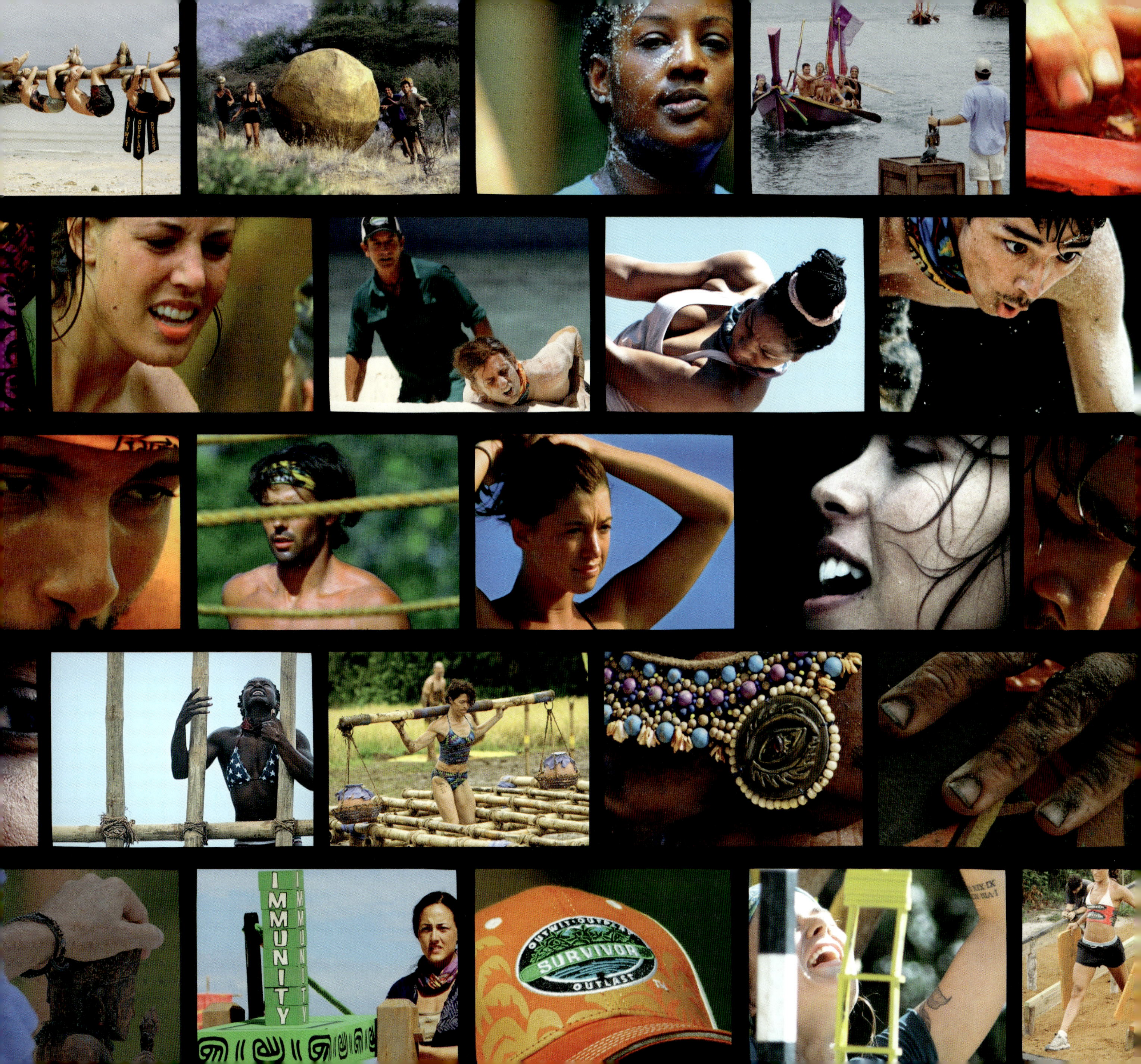

IMMUNITY

SURVIVOR
OUTLAST

OUTWIT

STAGE ONE

BALANCE BEAM

STAGE TWO

FRIGH
2
1
FINISH
FINISH
FINISH

OUTLAST

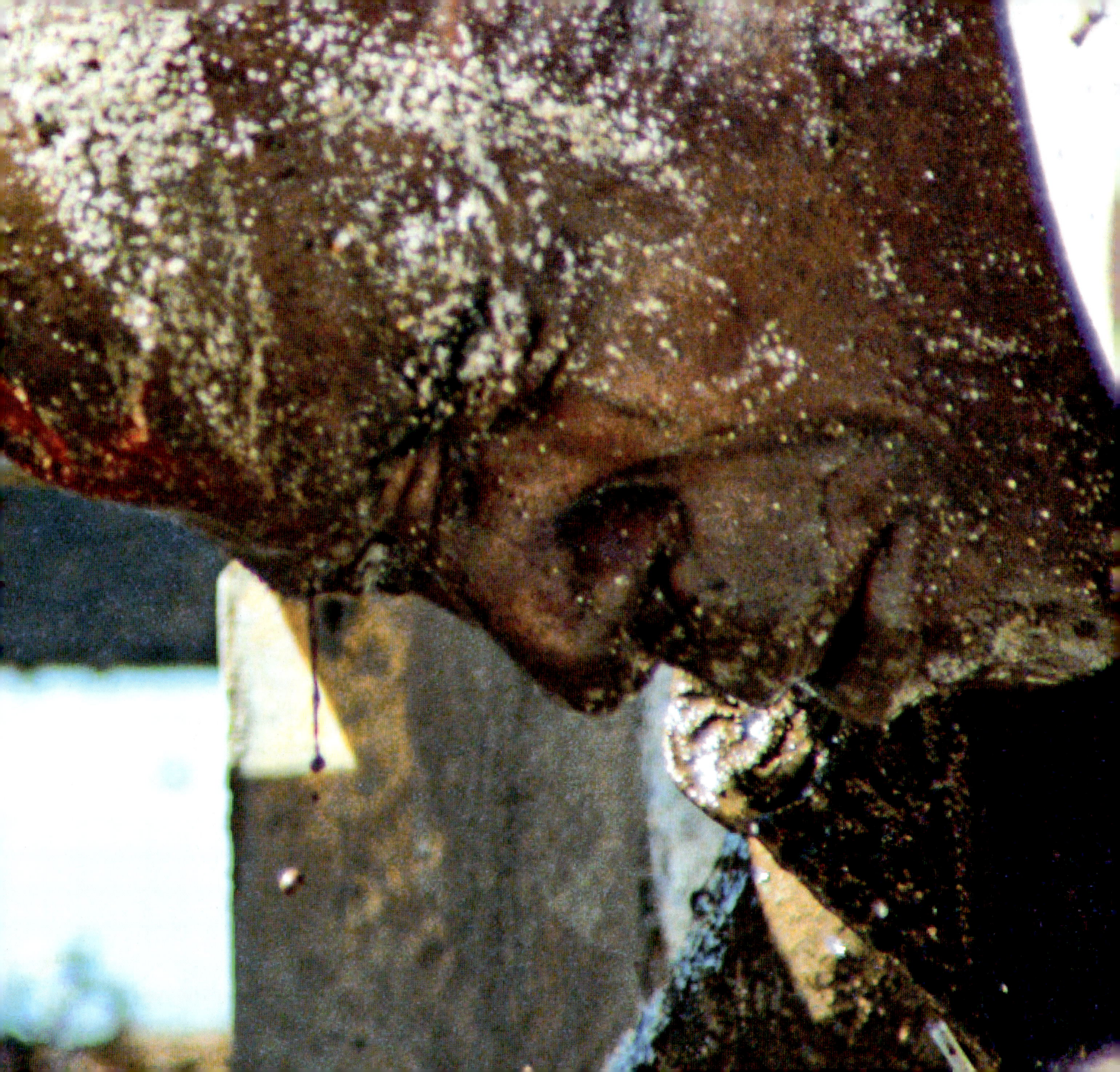

Every aspect of *Survivor* is real. From the jungle they live in, to the environment they must endure, to the challenges they compete in. And at times, the cumulative effect is simply overwhelming.

The most extreme example of this happened during *Survivor: Kaôh Rōng*, in Cambodia, on the hottest day I've ever experienced—115 degrees, with 100% humidity—when three players went down in the same challenge.

Debbie was the first to drop. I remember her saying, *"Like I'm on fire from the inside out,"* as our medical team rushed to cool her off with water and ice. We had no idea Debbie would be the least of the problems to come.

A challenge that seemed like it would never end finally did . . . and just moments later, Caleb dropped. Then Cydney.

From that moment forward, what happened was a chaotic blur—yet every second is carved into my memory.

It was instantly clear this was a very serious, life-threatening situation. Our medical team, led by Dr. Joe Rowles, quickly assessed both Cydney and Caleb. I remember yelling to our team: *"Everybody is now essential personnel!"*—meaning if you don't have a camera in your hand, find a way to help.

And that's exactly what happened. It was incredible. People sprinted for coolers, pouring water over Cydney and Caleb, packing ice anywhere we could—under arms, on chests, behind necks—anything to lower body temperature. When we ran out, we stripped every boat of its coolers and kept going.

Dream Teamers stood over them with umbrellas to block the sun. Players comforted one another. I remember our director, Dave Dryden, holding a huge block of ice on Caleb's chest with one hand while still calling out camera coverage with the other.

Our medical team quickly determined that Cydney, despite battling her painful heat exhaustion, was not in any immediate danger. So all the attention turned to Caleb, lying flat out and unresponsive. It is not hyperbole to say that Dr. Joe and his team had only one goal: keep Caleb alive.

I vividly remember kneeling next to Caleb as the medics put an oxygen mask over his face. IVs in both arms. Ice on his chest. Saline pouring in. But there was no breath. In the movies, when the oxygen mask goes on, the person breathes and they're okay. That didn't happen.

Dr. Joe and his team kept working. *"Caleb, can you hear me?"* No response. Again, *"Caleb, can you hear me?"* Nothing. Even though it was only 20 seconds, I can tell you that it felt like forever.

And then out of nowhere . . . one huge inhale and exhale. A single breath that seemed to pull him back from the edge. The color instantly returned and his cheeks filled out. It was one of the most incredible things I've ever witnessed.

And in that moment, I remember Dr. Joe, the definition of grace under pressure, giving the tiniest reaction . . . a simple breath of his own . . . that told me, *Caleb is going to be okay*.

Back at basecamp, our executive team had already alerted our helicopter pilot that we would be making an emergency evacuation. They had also already contacted a hospital in Phnom Penh and told them to expect us.

Caleb was never out of our care, and I am happy to say that he fully recovered and in fact came back to play *Survivor* again.

This moment happened more than 10 years ago, and this is the first time I've really ventured back into those memories to relive it. Even looking at these photos now, the memories are visceral and emotional. It was the most terrified I've ever been on *Survivor*. And ultimately the most proud I've ever been of our team.

It's a moment I will never forget. We'd been right at the edge—closer than anyone would ever want to venture—and we got through it, by staying calm and working together.

EJ 27 5782 6098•

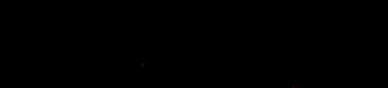

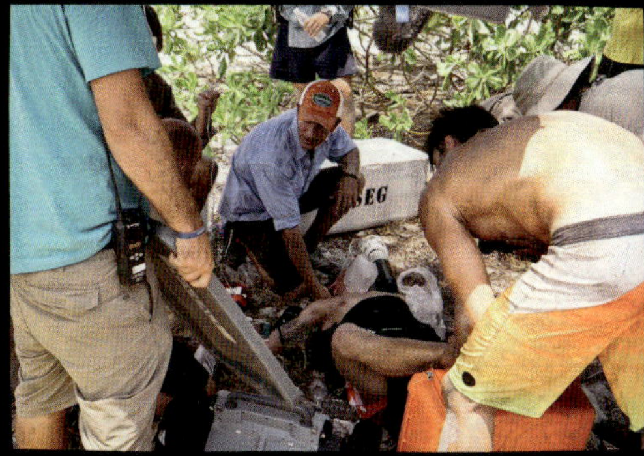

EJ 27 5782 609

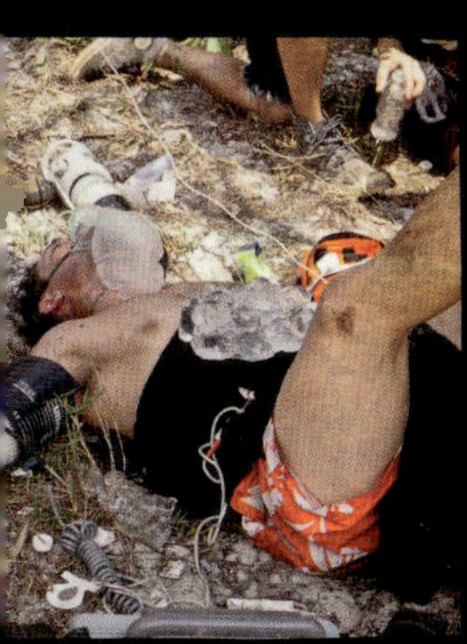

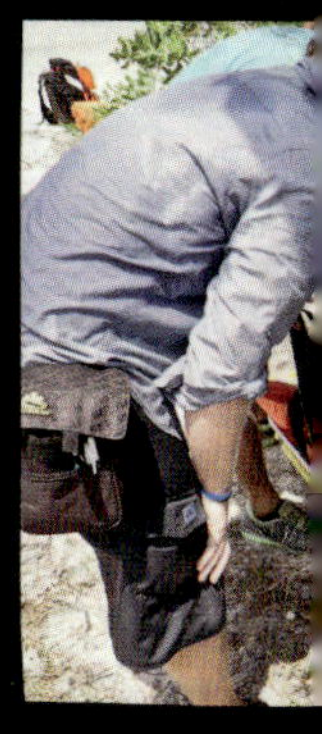

EJ 27 5782 6099+32 ●

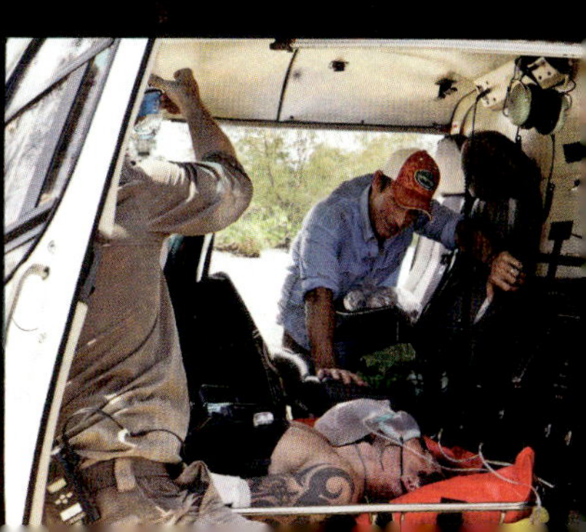

BEWARE ADVANTAGE!

CONGRATULATIONS!
YOU HAVE FOUND AN ADVANTAGE IN THE GAME
THIS IS AN IDOL NULLIFIER.
IT BLOCKS THE USE OF AN IDOL BY ANOTHER PLAYER.
HERE'S HOW IT WORKS...
YOU WILL PLAY THIS IN SECRET
WHEN YOU VOTE AT TRIBAL COUNCIL.
WRITE THE NAME OF THE PERSON
WANT TO BLOCK FROM USING AN IDOL
PERSON PLAYS AN IDOL FOR THEMSELVES
OR IF AN IDOL IS PLAYED FOR THEM,
THIS ADVANTAGE WILL NULLIFY THE IDOL
AND ANY VOTES CAST FOR THEM WILL COUNT.
AN IDOL IS NOT PLAYED FOR THAT PERSON,
THE NULLIFIER LOSES ITS POWER.
IT WILL REMAIN IN THE URN
AND NEVER BE SHOWN.
TIME WILL YOUR IDENTITY BE REVEALED.
PLACE THE NULLIFIER INSIDE YOUR VOTE
YOUR VOTE IN THE URN.

SECRET ADVANTAGE
CONGRATULATIONS!
YOU ARE IN THE FINAL THREE!!!
YOU HAVE ALSO WON AN ADVANTAGE
IN THE FORM OF INFORMATION.
AND YOU ARE THE ONLY ONE WHO KNOWS.
IN A FIRE MAKING CHALLENGE.
THE WINNER SECURES THE FINAL SEAT.
THE LOSER BECOMES
THE EIGHTH MEMBER OF THE JURY.
THERE IS A LOT OF STRATEGY
INVOLVED WITH YOUR DECISION.
YOU WILL SHARE THIS INFORMATION
AT THE BEGINNING OF TRIBAL.

YOUR ADVANTAGE
HAS BEEN PURCHASED.
THIS FIRE TOKEN
IS NOW YOURS.
Now for the part
it's so clear you've dreaded
Get ready to hike
to the council you're headed
Pack your bags
get ready to go
Which one it will be
the world will soon know
Even this dark cloud
has a small silver lining
The remaining seven
with fire will be dining

HIDDEN
YOU MUST EACH
CHOOSE AN URN

This is another great example of how time often offers a clearer picture of a past event.

These two photos were taken just moments after I told the players from *Survivor: Africa* that they would not be returning to their original camps. They were switching tribes.

We had never done anything like this before. No clue. No hint. Just a sudden, massive shift in direction. I remember a feeling of unease—even as I told them—because I could sense the players felt it was unfair.

Here they were, already living in the middle of Kenya—the most unforgiving environment we've ever shot *Survivor* in—playing a game in which they'd already built alliances and established trust . . . and now they were being forced to start over. And they didn't like it.

At the time, we saw it simply as a way to shake up the game. A twist for the sake of a twist.

But what I've come to understand more deeply, 25 years later, is how many of the choices we made in those early days came from instinct. Not a fully formed idea. Not a grand plan. Just a gut feeling we trusted.

It's a phrase we use a lot on *Survivor*: *Trust your gut.*

And that's exactly what we were doing as producers, even if we didn't yet understand why.

It's clear to me now that what we thought was a simple twist . . . was actually the opening of a creative door. A door that would eventually lead to dozens of different ways we could do the same thing: create uncertainty to force adaptation.

And what's most telling is that "Drop your buffs" is now one of the most iconic phrases in the history of the show. Every player knows what it means. And even though it brings tremendous uncertainty, they get excited when they hear it because they've learned to embrace the uncertainty.

It was never a question of fairness. It was simply the beginning of a new layer of *Survivor*.

One built on the idea that on *Survivor* . . . just like in life . . . nothing is ever permanent.

PERSON MUST GET ON THIS BOAT FOR
IF YOU CANNOT
WHOEVER DRAWS THE PURPLE ROCK
YOU WILL RETURN TO

FUJINON

WE ARE THE SURVIVOR IDOLS.

WE ARE NOT COMPETING.
WE DO NOT VOTE.
WE CANNOT WIN THE MILLION DOLLAR PRIZE.

OUR JOB IS TO MENTOR YOU IN THE GAME OF SURVIVOR
AND THEN OFFER YOU A CHANCE TO TEST WHAT YOU'VE LEARNED.

EVERYTHING THAT HAPPENS HERE IS INTENDED TO MAKE
YOU A BETTER SURVIVOR PLAYER.

ONE BAD DECISION
CAN HAUNT YOU
FOREVER

R TORCH
EXTINCTI
THIS IS THE EDGE OF EXTINCTION.
YOU WILL HAVE TO WORK HARD FOR EVERYTHING.
WHEN FEAR OR LONELINESS SETS IN,
YOU MUST FIND THE RESOLVE TO OVERCOME.
IF YOU ARE INDUSTRIOUS, YOU CAN EARN FIRE TOKENS
TO HELP YOU GET BACK IN THE GAME.
IF AT ANY POINT YOU WISH TO END YOUR ADVENTURE,
RAISE THE SAIL AND A BOAT WILL PICK YOU UP.
EXTINCTION

TRIBAL

This is the place you fear—and the place you chase.

The fire draws you in. It always has.
It lights the path to judgment. To truth. To the end.

Tribal Council knows how far you've come.
It knows what you sacrificed to get here.

But it also knows this:
Stakes are everything.
And without them, the journey would mean nothing.

So this is where it all comes to bear.
The hunger. The hardship. The storms. The bonds.
Every challenge.
Every risk you took to stay alive.
And the choices you made when no one was watching.
All of it—laid bare in the firelight.

This is where torches are snuffed.
Where games are shattered and dreams die.

But not for all.
For Tribal Council is also where legends are made.

This is the final threshold.
This is where you claim your victory.
And if your flame survives . . . your story will burn forever.

"TRIBAL COUNCIL"
MARCH 8, 2000

STILL FIVE DAYS OUT. THIS SHOW IS SO MUCH BIGGER THAN I INITIALLY UNDERSTOOD.

I AM PUTTING ALL OF MY INTENTION & ATTENTION INTO THE CLIMAX OF THE SHOW CALLED TRIBAL COUNCIL.

TRIBAL COUNCIL SHOULD FEEL LIKE A RITUAL THAT HAS BEEN GOING ON FOR YEARS... AND YEARS... AND YEARS.

WE WANT TO CREATE A NEW VERNACULAR. A NEW WORLD.

MYTHIC.

MARCH 10, 2000

JUST DID OUR FIRST WALK-THRU OF TRIBAL. IT'S INCREDIBLY EXCITING.

NEVER ANYTHING LIKE IT.
NOTHING.

IT'S GOING TO BE SO REAL. SO RAW.
BUT I CAN'T BELIEVE MARK IS STILL "FINDING" THE SHOW. HE SEEMS FEARLESS IN THAT HE DOESN'T SEEM WORRIED THAT WE ARE STILL FIGURING OUT HOW IT WILL WORK. EVERYBODY ON THE CREW HAS IDEAS & HE IS OPEN TO ALL OF THEM.
EVEN LAST MINUTE IDEAS. INTOXICATING.
DISCUSSED "FIRE REPRESENTS LIFE" & BLUE LIGHTS FOR PLAYER EXIT.

RICH

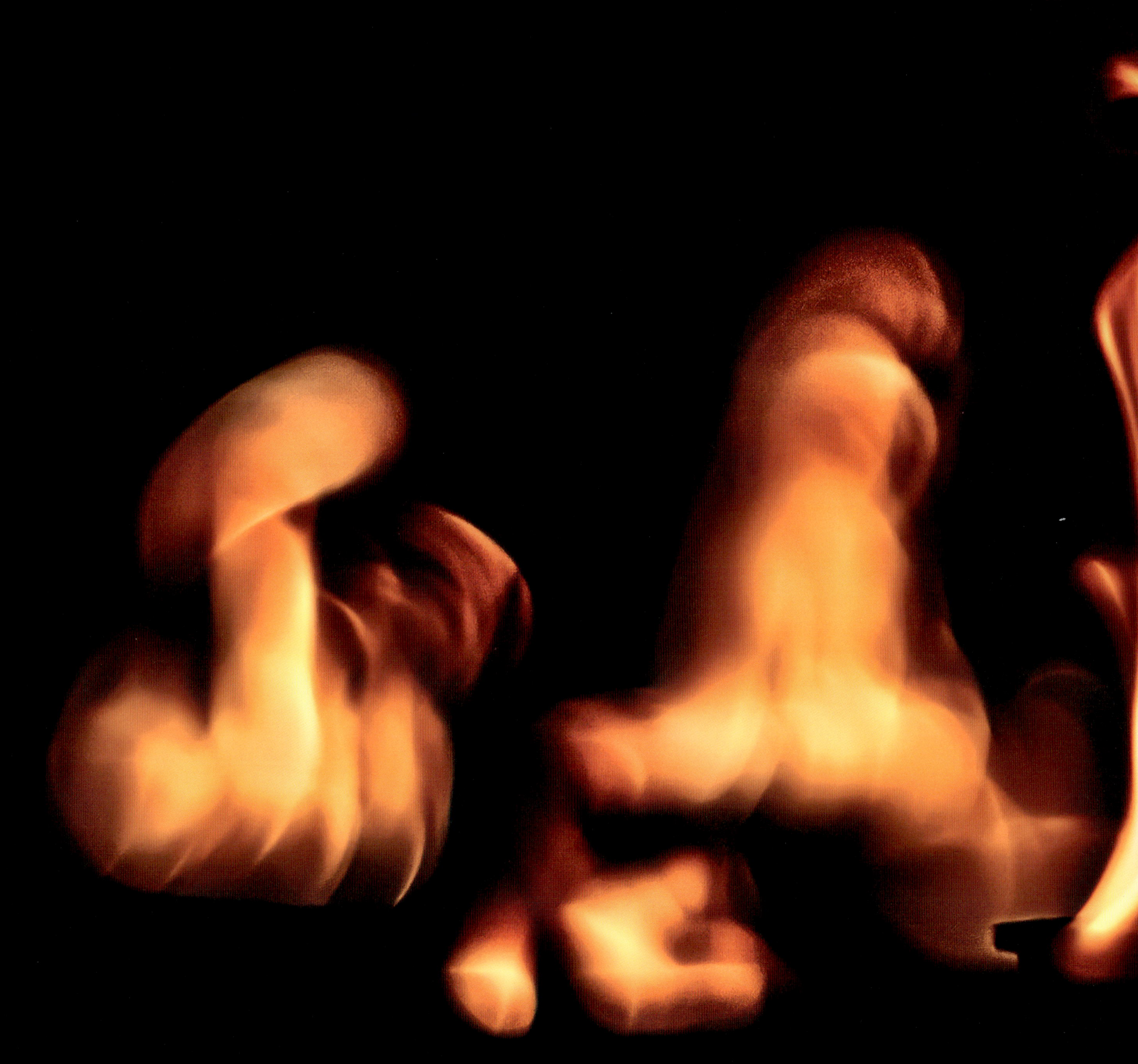

TRIBAL
COUNCIL
SURVIVOR

Erinn
Laura

Phillip

I ♥ ROB
ONE SU

RVIVOR

THE RETURN

The game is over. The torches are out. And for the first time in weeks, the players begin the journey back to the world they left behind.

They carry more than just memories . . . they carry the lessons, scars, and triumphs earned in the jungle.

Saying goodbye to the island means stepping into a new life, shaped by everything they've endured.

Some can't wait to go home. Others would give anything for one more day.

But all of them leave changed.

I don't need to see my face in this photo to know what I'm thinking.
It's the same thing I think at the end of every season:
Did we deliver what we promised?
Did we give them what they came for?

From the beginning, *Survivor* has been an invitation:
Leave your ordinary world. Step into the unknown. Say yes.
And if you're willing to do that—if you're truly willing to say yes—
then we'll give everything we have to deliver the adventure of a lifetime.
That's the deal.

So when I look at this photo,
I'm not thinking about the show.
I'm thinking about the players . . . and the world they're stepping back into.
Because one thing is certain: When you say yes to *Survivor*, you never return the same.

You may go home more grounded. More confident. More open.
A better friend, a more present parent.
You may carry a deeper trust in others, or in yourself.

You may discover you're capable of more than you ever imagined . . .
or that you're as good as you'd always hoped.

When you leave behind comfort and step forward
with only courage and curiosity, something shifts.
You go home carrying that shift with you.
You'll see it reflected in the eyes of others . . . because they won't look at you the same.
You aren't the same.

That's what I'm thinking about when I stare at that ocean.
Not the fear.
Not the hunger.
Not the blindsides.
I'm thinking about the players.
The risk they took.
The change they made.
And the new life that's waiting for them—when they return.

SURVIVOR

And every time a season ends, I think about those original 16 players—the ones who stepped onto that beach with nothing to guide them but their courage and curiosity. They helped launch this adventure without a map, without a blueprint, and without a single guarantee that any of it would work.

Which is why, when I think back on the past 25 years, one word rises above the rest: *trust*.

When *Survivor* premiered, back in the summer of 2000, nothing like it had ever existed. No template. Nothing to follow. It was a very different, very risky, and very grand idea that required a giant leap of faith.

And that leap required trust. A lot of it.

The network trusted Mark.
Mark trusted his team—the storytellers, the crew, the host, the cinematographers—all of us charged with bringing this new kind of adventure to life.

Those players trusted us.
And we trusted you—the viewer—to take this ride with us.

Yes, it all sounded strange at first. "The tribe has spoken." "Fire represents life." But that was the point. We wanted to create something that felt mythic and ancient. A world with its own rules, its own rituals, its own language.
A world that was new to you but felt as though it had been around for centuries.

And we didn't just say it. We shot it that way. With firelight and shadows. Tight close-ups that revealed truth. Epic wides that captured the scale of the jungle and the vulnerability of the player. Sweat, tears, saturated colors—all pushed to the edge.

It was bold. It was cinematic.
And it was unabashed in its pursuit of authenticity.

Without trust, it could never work.
But with trust, amazing things can happen.

I believe trust is the most significant reason *Survivor* worked then and continues to work today, because we all believe in it.

That's why we're still here, 25 years later.

On behalf of everyone who has ever worked on *Survivor* and every person who has ever played, I offer a heartfelt thank-you for trusting us.

Without you, we would not still be here.

—Jeff

IT'S WILD TO LOOK BACK OVER 25 YEARS OF *SURVIVOR*...KNOWING IT ALMOST NEVER HAPPENED.

It took over a year of pitching *Survivor* to various networks before it finally found a home at CBS.

The last step in closing the deal was deciding who would host the show. Once I'd made my decision, I told Leslie Moonves, the CEO of CBS, "I'd like to hire Jeff Probst." He said, "Great. We have a deal. Thirteen episodes, CBS Primetime, no pilot."

I left his office elated. But as I rode the elevator down to the parking garage and got into my Land Rover, another feeling started creeping in . . . panic. I knew I was a good salesman, but I'd never produced a show like this—and I didn't know where to start.

Fortunately, cell phones didn't exist, because if they had, I might have called Leslie right then and said, "I'm sorry, you've given me this incredible opportunity, but I don't want to let you or myself down."

I sat in that parking lot for half an hour, but the thought of going back upstairs to tell Leslie *"no"* was so daunting that, instead, I decided to keep moving forward.

So I drove to a library and started pulling books on islands from around the world. I stumbled across a VHS National Geographic documentary called *The Eagle and the Snake*, about the venomous sea snakes on Snake Island in Pulau Tiga. I thought it looked just dangerous enough that it could work for *Survivor*.

The next day I cold-called the Malaysian tourism board and pitched them on this incredible opportunity to promote Malaysia through a prime-time CBS TV show. They were intrigued enough to fly me first class to Kuala Lumpur, where a helicopter and scout team were waiting to show me Pulau Tiga—the very spot where we shot the first season of *Survivor* more than 25 years ago.

And the rest is history.

I never imagined *Survivor* would last this long or lead to so many incredible, life-changing adventures. It changed my life in ways I could never have predicted, and I'm grateful for every single moment of it.

—Mark Burnett

I've been with *Survivor* since the very beginning... when this wild, crazy, untested idea first came to life. It was an honor and a thrill to be given the opportunity to help shape the visual language for a brand-new kind of show. Twenty-five years later, I'm still here... one of many cinematographers lucky enough to bring these stories to life.

On *Survivor*, we're given a rare gift: the freedom... and the encouragement... to push boundaries, take risks, and chase bold new ideas. We're urged to experiment, to try things that might not work, and to keep searching for fresh ways to elevate the stories of these remarkable humans through our lenses. That spirit of trust and adventure brings out the best in all of us... because we're not just individuals; we're a team, united by one goal: to capture the story in the most powerful, cinematic way possible.

Survivor has never been about the camera gear we use. It's always been about the eyes behind the lens... the unique point of view each cinematographer brings to their work. I felt that every day as I sifted through millions of images and hundreds of hard drives to create this book.

Not every cinematographer listed here has an image in the book... but every single one has shaped the look, feel, and heartbeat of *Survivor*. And every photo you see carries the trust, style, and perspective they helped create.

It's an honor to be part of this extraordinary team. We hope you've enjoyed this book as much as we've enjoyed capturing the moments within it.

—Scott Duncan

RS
001/00:09:02.365
Mag Recording Raw T5
BOX 211 F
16624
300f/s
45°
2048x1080

THE CINEMATOGRAPHERS WHO HAVE BROUGHT *SURVIVOR* TO LIFE FOR 25 YEARS

DIRECTOR OF PHOTOGRAPHY Scott Duncan · **DIRECTORS OF PHOTOGRAPHY–REALITY** Derek Carver · Peter Wery · Michael Murrey · **DIRECTOR OF PHOTOGRAPHY–SECOND UNIT** Russ Fill · **DIRECTORS OF AERIAL PHOTOGRAPHY** David Arnold · Christopher Barker · Chris Chanda · Mark Hryma · Granger Scholtz · **DIRECTOR OF PHOTOGRAPHY, CHALLENGES** Peter Pescell · **DIRECTOR OF PHOTOGRAPHY, CHALLENGES & TRIBAL COUNCIL** Mark "Ninja" Lynch · **DIRECTOR OF PHOTOGRAPHY, UNDERWATER** Lance Milbrand · **SENIOR DRONE OPERATOR** Nic Van Der Westhuizen · **DRONE OPERATORS** Ryan Hermosura · Kenny Hoffmann · Dwight Winston · **CINEFLEX OPERATOR** Gray Mitchell · **CAMERA OPERATORS** Jorge Alves Jr. · Cullum Andrews · George Andrews · Graham Andrews · Michael Applebaum · John Armstrong · Tim Barker · Kathryn Barrows · Josh Bartel · Len Beard · Marc Bennett · James Boon · Rory Boon · Biff Bracht · Fabio Cascao · Paulo Castillo · David Chapiro · Rodney Chauvin · Jonathan Chinn · Lanza Coffin · Sam Collins · Cirio "Bong" Conde · Luke Cormack · Tom Cowan · Tony Croll · Bennie Cronje · Richard Dallett · Michael Dean · Leighton DeBarros · Michael Dillon · Lee Doig · Randall Einhorn · Chris Ellison · Glenn Louis Evans · Dan Foster · David J. Frederick · Eric Freeburg · Ben Gamble · Jimmy Garland · Kevin Garrison · Nixon George · Raj Gibson · Tom Gleeson · Ryan Godard · Chad Griepentrog · Brandon Haberman · Shana Hagan · Jim Harrington · Kent Harvey · Nathanial Havholm · Marcus Hebbelmann · Rick Higgs · Derek Hoffmann · Matthias Hoffmann · Toby Hogan · Derek Holt · Jay Hunter · Jude Jatau · Dionne Jones · Efrain "Mofi" Laguna · Per Larsson · Rich Lerner · David Linstrom · Alistair Lyne · Brian D. Marleau · Michael "Mac" McAleenan · Kyle McAuley · Sean McKelvey · Andrew Metz · Ian Miller · Barnaby Mitchell · Vince Monteleone · Ryan Mooney · Paul Moss · Sarah Natoli · Barry Nichols · Nico Nyoni · Ryan O'Donnell · Jojo Oducayen · Johann Oosthuizen · Paul Peddinghaus · Peter Pescell · Jeff Phillips · Jesse Phinney · Alan Pierce · Peter Pilafian · Nejc Poberaj · Daniel Powell · Louis Powell · Thomas Pretorius · Jonathan Price · Jack Reichart · Jeff Rhoads · Dax Rhorer · Jack Richard · Jovan Sales · David M. Sammons · Scott Sandman · Erick Sarmiento · Jeremy Schneider · David Shapiro · Matt Shelly · Peter Sheppard · Raphael Smadja · Chris Smith · Owen Smith · Matthew Sohn · Dirk Steyn · Jeff Streich · David Sullivan · John Tattersall · Jeffrey Taylor · Holly Thompson · Martin Unversaw · Paulo Velozo · David Vlastis · George Waterman · Jeff Watt · Paul Webb · Fed Wetherbee · Mande Whitaker · Jeff Wilkins · Michael Yelseth · **CAMERA ASSISTANTS** Luiz Abrahao · Isaura Afonson · Simon Alltoft · Venetia Armstrong-Smith · Jay Arnette · Jason Arthur · Jon Attenborough · Jeremy Austin · Marcus

Ballantine · Brett Barlee · Ines Barlerin · Duncan Barrett · Brandon Batten · Alex Bayne · Luke Bennett · Ilya Berenson · Clark Bernstein · Brett Brolliar · Beau Brooks · Terry Brown · Bryan Butt · Oliver Caldow · Chris Camp · Chas Carlson · Jay Carreras · Dave Casella · Dylan Cashbaugh · Sheldon Casimir · Roland Castro · Justin Causer · Daion Chesney · Anderson Collins · Javier Costa · Geoffrey Costello · Jim Costello · Patrick Costello · Keith Cox · Robert Croll · Max Curtis · Jamie Daubney · Andrew Davis · John Davis · Sam Dunwoody · Skye Ebden · Patrick Ebert · Caleb Einhorn · Willem Engelbrecht · Ezra Epwell · Martin Fargher · Louis Fehlig · Eddie Flandez · Michael Francis · Brent Freeburg · Piers Freeman · Elvira Garcia · Matt Gaumer · Jennifer Gear · Georgio · Chris Gibson · Hayden Gilmour · Peter Goetz · Francisco Gomes · Jorge Gonzalez · Jose Gonzalez · Scott Goode · Andrew Greenan · Gerhard Greyling · Nic Greyling · Xavier Hale · Scott Hanlon · Zack Hannon · Darren Hao · Craig Harrison · Connor Hopkins · Ubonrat Hubler · John Iacoangelo · Kelly Jacobson · Joe Janes · Oscar Jimenez · Nehemiah Joseph · Vonna Keller · Chris Kelly · Joseph Keseokile · Danny Kodesh · Maria Koroiveibau · Jeff Kubach · Rowell Laguna · Scott Last · Edison Layne · Gerald Lee · Jose Leite · David Lindsay · Jason Liquori · Kiana Liu · Terrance Lofton Jr. · Shadley Lombard · Mark Lott · Angelo Lovato · Kristian Mackie · Melissa Mahoney · Justin Mangus · Jone Marayawa · Devon Mardyks · Abe Martinez · Chris Mayer-Hohdahl · Cliff McCall · Aeron McKeough · Andrew McPherson · Lobsang Tenzin Meindrukbhuk · Beto Mello · Shannon Metelko · David Mickler · Ben Milward-Bason · Santiago Montoya · Pierre Morton · Chris Mossier · Everette Motta · Kisi Mtshiselo · Thomas Mueller · Riley Munday · Nathan Mundel · Stuart Murray · Tanuj Naicker · Yee Wili Pita Nawaqavou · Peter Neilsen · Andrew Netboy · Donald Ng · JJ Osborne · Rob Osburn · James Pages · Norwood Palta · Stephan Palz · Timothy Panaino · Kalpech Panchal · Emma Pantell · Rowan Peacock · Geerick Pepler · Joanna Perdue · Hernan Perez · Sam Pietsch · Dave Pile · Eric Pinho · Paolo Pollono · Damien Prestidge · Falko Purner · Ratu Savenaca Qalova · Sherli Quinn · Mary Raela · Addison Rafford · Vilikesa Ramaqa · Dave Ranftle · Paula Raqeukai Koroimata · Jamal Reeves · Riley Reiss · Darlene Richardson · Nicole Ritterstein · Rob Robertson · Sean Robinson · Rodrigo Rodrigues · Kurt Rolle · Jacy Roman · Rob Sackett · Omar Saleem · Chan Samson · Brett Sanson · Melvin Santacruz · Jimmy Saqanatoto · Dave Schwander · Gary Shaffer · Matt Shelly · Michael Short · Dylan Silk · Adam Sitta · Steven Smalley · Jacob Smith · Paul Smith · Stroube Smith · Chuck Snyder · Ilan Sollamy · Isireli S. Sorovakatini · Brian Stevens · Nicholas Stewart · Steele Stride · Adam Szulewski · Randy Taylor · Jacob Teixeira · Mpho Tekane · Luke Terbieten · Weerapong Tharneerat · Lawrence Joe Thomsen · James Todd · Kylie Topal · Paul Tran · Michael Troy · Bram Tulloch · Katie Uhlaender · Steve Van Dis · Piyasak Veratrakul · Joey Vetere · Shawn Viens · Josefa Waqa · Vince Warburton · Jone Weisblatt · Pedro Wery · Timoci Wilisoni · Zach Zaleski

PHOTO INDEX

Survivor: Borneo

Survivor: Thailand
Erin Collins

Survivor: Palau

Survivor: Borneo

Survivor: Cambodia—Second Chance

Survivor: Borneo

Survivor: 49
Fiji

Survivor: All-Stars
Pearl Islands, Panama

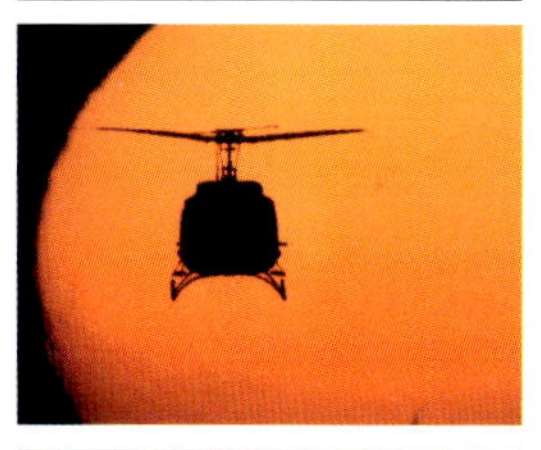

Survivor: 50
Fiji

Survivor: Heroes vs. Healers vs. Hustlers
Fiji

Survivor: Australia

Survivor: Cook Islands

Survivor: Palau

Survivor: Redemption Island
San Juan del Sur, Nicaragua
Photo: Monty Brinton

By Land, By Sea, By Air
Survivor: Africa, Heroes vs. Villains (Parvati Shallow), ***Ghost Island*** (Photo: Robert Voets)

Survivor: 49
Fiji
Sophie Segreti, Kristina Mills, Jason Truel, Michelle "MC" Chukwujekwu

Survivor: Winners at War
Fiji
Photo: Robert Voets

The Buff Is Proof
Survivor: Micronesia, 48 Fiji, Philippines, Millennials vs. Gen X, Nicaragua, Winners at War, David vs. Goliath

Survivor 50
Fiji

Survivor: Brains vs. Brawn vs. Beauty
Kaôh Rōng
Photo: Robert Voets

Survivor: Cook Islands

Survivor: Brains vs. Brawn vs. Beauty
Kaôh Rōng
Photo: Monty Brinton

Survivor: Marquaseas, Palau, David vs. Goliath, Edge of Extinction

Survivor: Island of the Idols
Fiji

Survivor: Borneo

Survivor 43
Fiji

Survivor 43
Fiji

Survivor: Borneo

Survivor: David vs. Goliath
Fiji

Survivor: Cambodia—Second Chance

Survivor 50
Fiji

Survivor 49
Fiji

Survivor: Fiji
James Reid, Mookie Lee, Jessica deBen, and Earl Cole
Photo: Monty Brinton

Survivor: Borneo
Jenna Lewis
Photo: Monty Brinton

Survivor: Panama, Marquaseas (Sarah Jones), ***Tocantins, Borneo*** (Jenna Lewis)

Survivor: Winners at War
Fiji
Tony Vlachos
Photo: Robert Voets

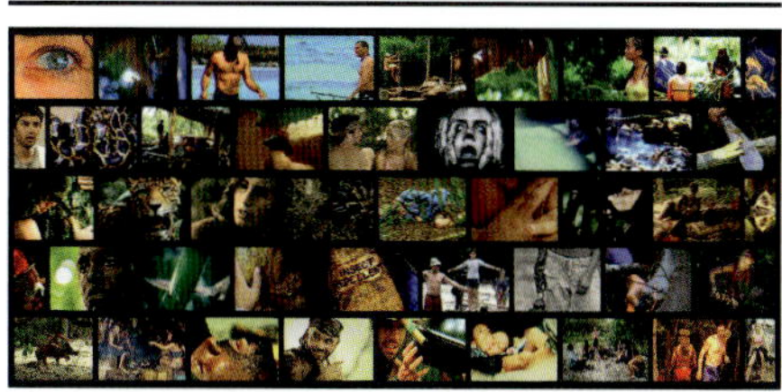

The Jungle Offers No Welcome

Survivor: Brains vs. Brawn vs. Beauty
Kaôh Rōng
Tai Trang

Survivor: Redemption Island
San Juan Del Sur, Nicaragua
Andrea Boehlke

Survivor: Blood vs Water
San Juan Del Sur, Nicaragua

Survivor: David vs. Goliath
Fiji

Survivor: Tocantins

Survivor: Thailand
Jed Hildebrand

Survivor: Australia

Survivor: Australia

Survivor: Winners at War
Ben Driebergen, Michele Fitzgerald

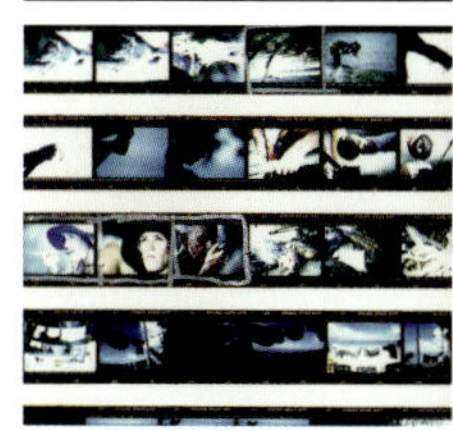

Survivor: Borneo

Survivor: Heroes vs. Villains
Upolu, Samoa

Survivor: All Stars, Winners at War
Amber Mariano & Boston Rob Mariano

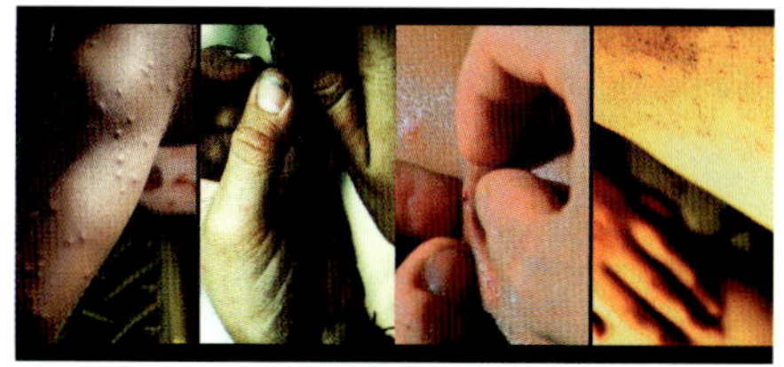

Survivor: Marquesas, Borneo, Guatemala, Australia

Survivor: Tocantins
The Brazilian Highlands
Scott Duncan
J. T. Thomas
Photo Left by: Abe Martinez

Survivor 49
Fiji

Survivor 49
Fiji

Survivor: All-Stars
Pearl Islands, Panama
Rupert Boneham

Survivor 49
Fiji

Survivor 49
Fiji

Survivor 50
Fiji
Dee Valladares

Survivor 44
Fiji

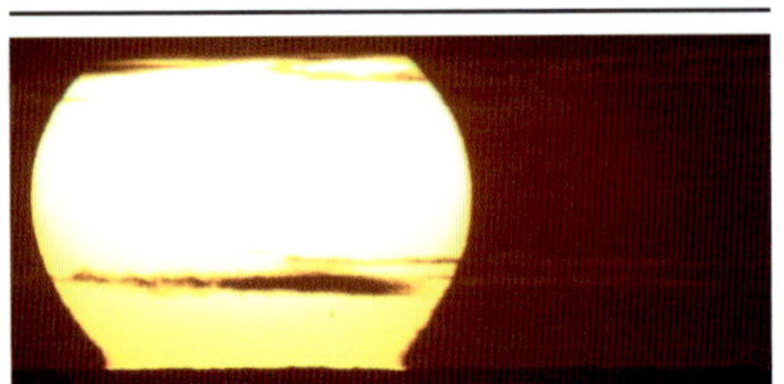

Survivor 43
Fiji

Survivor 41
Fiji
Erika Casupanan

Survivor 47
Fiji

Survivor: All-Stars
Pearl Islands, Panama
Amber Mariano, Boston Rob Mariano, Ethan Zohn, Jenna Lewis, Jerri Manthey

Every Moment, a Test

Survivor 44
Fiji

Survivor: Brains vs. Brawn vs. Beauty
Kaôh Rōng
Gondol Tribe: Julia Sokolowski, Tai Trang, Anna Khait, Caleb Reynolds, Nick Maiorano, Michele Fitzgerald

Survivor: 45 (Fiji), ***44*** (Fiji), ***Pearl Islands, 43*** (Fiji)

Survivor: Australia
Photo: Monty Brinton

Survivor 49
Fiji
Savannah Louie

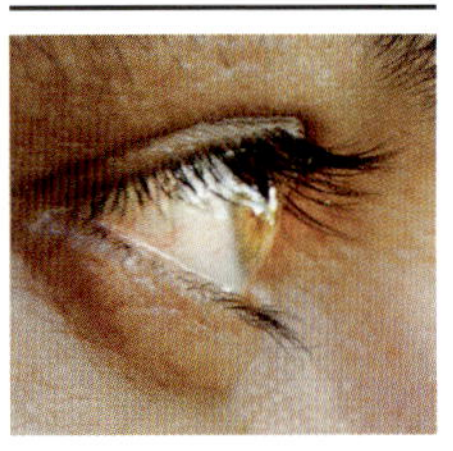

Survivor: Island of the Idols
Fiji
Sandra Diaz-Twine

Survivor: Heroes vs. Healers vs. Hustlers

Survivor 47
Fiji

Survivor: Australia
Michael Skupin, Jerri Manthey

Survivor 45
Fiji

Survivor 45
Fiji
Emily Flippen

Survivor 42
Fiji
Jonathan Young, Maryanne Oketch

Survivor: Winners at War
Fiji
Nick Wilson, Yul Kwon

Survivor 44
Fiji

Survivor 43
Fiji

Survivor: Guatemala, China
Danni Boatwright (photo: Monty Brinton), Ashley Massaro

Survivor 49
Fiji
Kristina Mills

Survivor: Gabon

Survivor 49
Fiji
Sage Ahrens-Nichols

Players Test Themselves

Survivor 45
Fiji
Kaleb Gebrewold

Survivor: Palau
Katie Gallagher, Ian Rosenberger, Tom Westman

Survivor: Palau
Katie Gallagher, Ian Rosenberger, Tom Westman

Survivor 42
Fiji
Jonathan Young

Survivor: Cook Islands
Jonathan Penner, Parvati Shallow
Photo: Bill Inoshita

Survivor: Worlds Apart
Joe Anglim
Photo: Robert Voets

Survivor: Micronesia—Fans vs. Favorites
Natalie Bolton
Photo: Monty Brinton

Survivor: Fiji
Andria “Dreams” Herd
Photo: Jeffrey R. Staab

Survivor 46
Fiji
Tiffany Ervin

Survivor: Island of the Idols
Fiji
Aaron Meredith

Survivor: David vs. Goliath
Jeremy Crawford

More Than Strength

Survivor: Pearl Islands
Mark Burnett, Jeff Probst

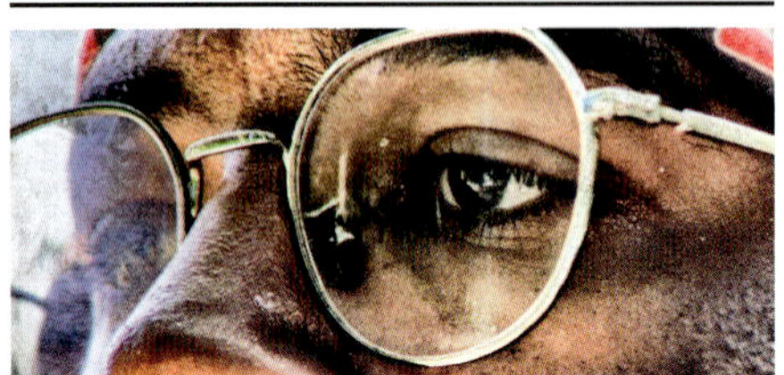

Survivor 49
Fiji
Jawan Pitts

Survivor: Africa
Photo: Robert Voets

No One Walks Away Untouched

Survivor: Australia
Mark Burnett

Survivor: Australia

Survivor: Australia

Survivor 49
Fiji

Survivor: Nicaragua
Brenda Lowe, Kelly Shinn
Photos: Monty Brinton

Survivor 45
Fiji
Dee Valladares

Survivor: Island of the Idols
Jack Nichting, Jamal Shipman
Survivor: Winners at War
Jeremy Collins
Survivor: Guatemala
Judd Sergeant

Survivor: Heroes vs. Healers vs. Hustlers
Chrissy Hofbeck, Ben Driebergen, Alan Ball, Ashley Nolan

Survivor: Borneo
Richard Hatch, Kelly Wiglesworth, Rudy Boesch
Photos: Monty Brinton

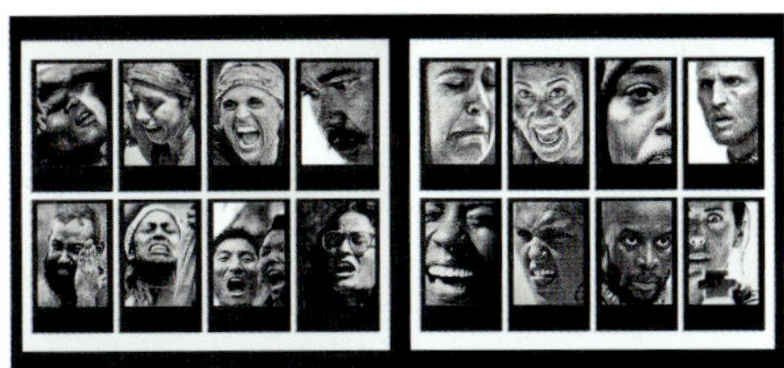

Pain and Triumph Walk Side by Side

Survivor: David vs. Goliath
Fiji
Bi Nguyen

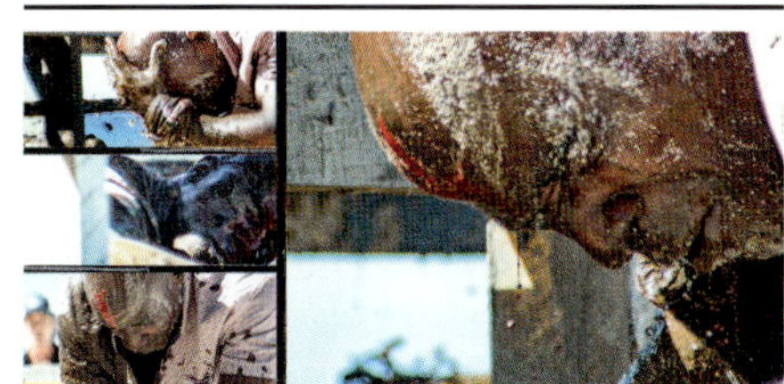

Survivor 44
Fiji
Bruce Perreault

Survivor: Brains vs. Brawn vs. Beauty
Kaôh Rōng

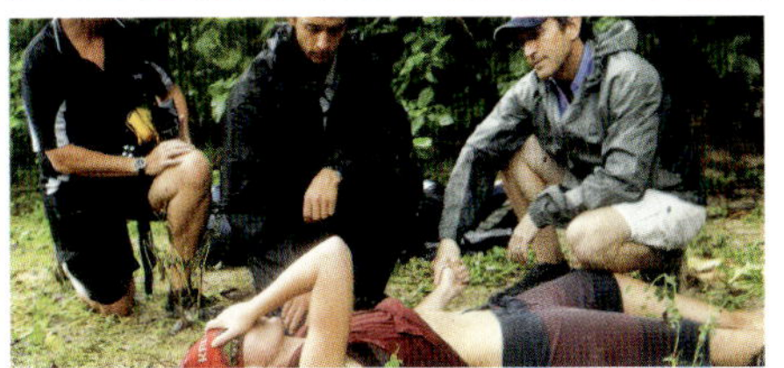

Survivor: Philippines
Dana Lambert
Photo: Monty Brinton

Survivor 48
Fiji
Joe Hunter, Eva Erickson
Photo: Robert Voets

Some Emerge Forged

Survivor 43
Fiji

Survivor: David vs. Goliath
Fiji
Photo:
Robert Voets

Survivor: Heroes vs. Healers vs. Hustlers
Chrissy Hofbeck

Survivor: Worlds Apart
San Juan del Sur, Nicaragua
Jenn Brown

Survivor: Worlds Apart
San Juan del Sur, Nicaragua

Survivor: Fans vs. Favorites
Micronesia
Cirie Fields
Photo: Jeffrey R. Staab

Survivor: Winners at War
Sandra Diaz-Twine

Survivor: Micronesia
Ozzy Lusth

The Path Is Never Straight for Long

Survivor: Africa
Photos: Monty Brinton

Survivor 47
Fiji
Andy Rueda, Teeny Chirichillo, Caroline Vidmar

Survivor 45
Fiji
Austin Li Coon, Emily Flippen, Katurah Topps

Survivor 44
Fiji
Emily Flippen

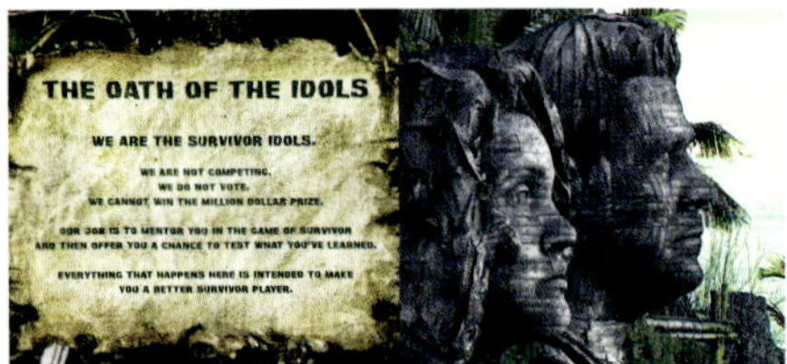

Survivor: Island of the Idols
Fiji

Survivor: Tocantins
Benjamin "Coach" Wade
Photo: Monty Brinton

Survivor: Ghost Island
Fiji

Survivor: Ghost Island
Fiji
Photo: Michele Crowe

Survivor: Redemption Island
Matt Elrod, Francesca Hogi
Photo: Monty Brinton

Survivor: Edge of Extinction, Winners at War

Survivor: Heroes vs. Healers vs. Hustlers
Alan Ball
Survivor: Winners at War
Ethan Zohn
Photos: Robert Voets

Survivor: Edge of Extinction
Keith Sowell
Photo:
Robert Voets

Survivor 50
Fiji

Survivor 44
Fiji

Survivor 48
Fiji

Survivor 47
Fiji

Survivor: Fiji

Survivor: David vs. Goliath
Fiji

Survivor 49
Fiji

Survivor: Borneo

Survivor: Australia
Jeff Probst, Mark Burnett
Photo: Monty Brinton

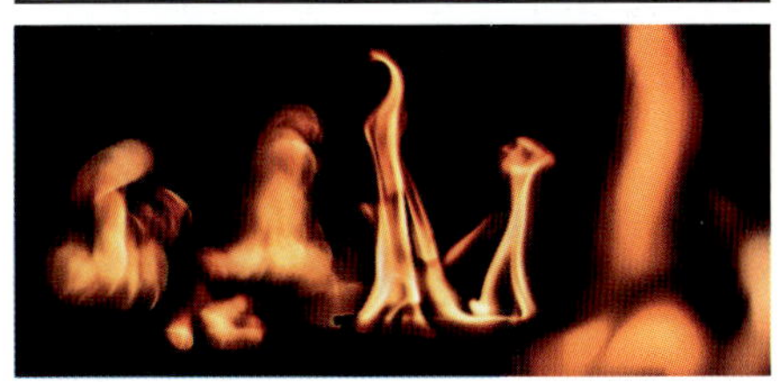

Survivor 49
Fiji

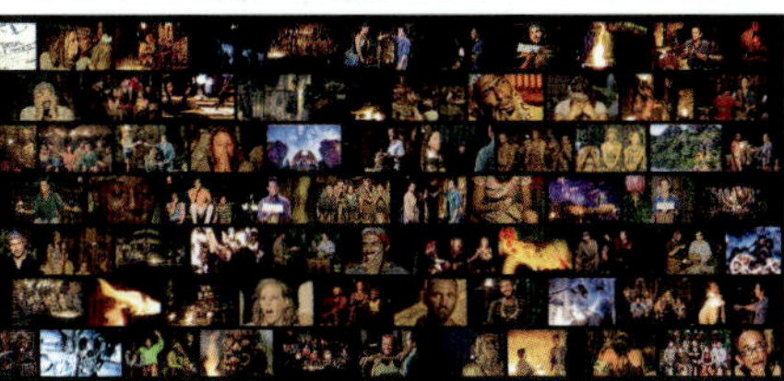

This Is the Place You Fear—and the Place You Chase

Survivor: Fans vs. Favorites
Micronesia
Photos: Monty Brinton

Survivor: Fans vs. Favorites
Caramoan
Photos: Greg Gayne

Survivor: All Stars
Pearl Islands, Panama

Survivor 47
Fiji
Rachel LaMont, Genevieve Mushaluk, Andy Rueda, Teeny Chirichillo

Survivor 49
Fiji

Fire Represents Your Life

One Survivor

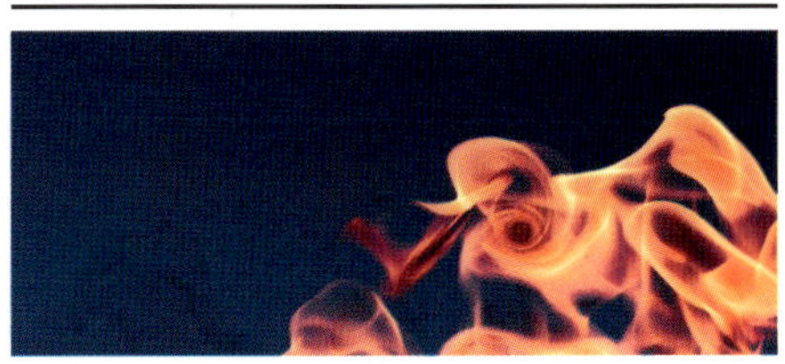

Survivor 50
Fiji

Survivor 49
Fiji

Survivor: Borneo

Survivor: Borneo
Stacey Stillman, Gervase Peterson, Jenna Lewis, Rudy Boesch, Sean Kenniff, Colleen Haskell, Ramona Gray, Susan Hawk, Greg Buis, Kelly Wiglesworth, Dirk Been, Richard Hatch, Sonja Christopher, Joel Klug, B.B. Andersen, Gretchen Cordy

Survivor 50
Fiji

Survivor: Australia
Mark Burnett

Survivor 50
Fiji
Scott Duncan

Survivor 50
Fiji

Simon & Schuster
1230 Avenue of the Americas
New York, NY 10020

First Simon & Schuster hardcover edition February 2026

Book Design & Photo Curation: Mackenzie Oravec
Book Producer: Sarah Newcomb-Butt

Manufactured in Canada

1 3 5 7 9 10 8 6 4 2

Library of Congress Control Number has been applied for.

ISBN 978-1-6682-2220-1
ISBN 978-1-6682-3214-9 (ebook)

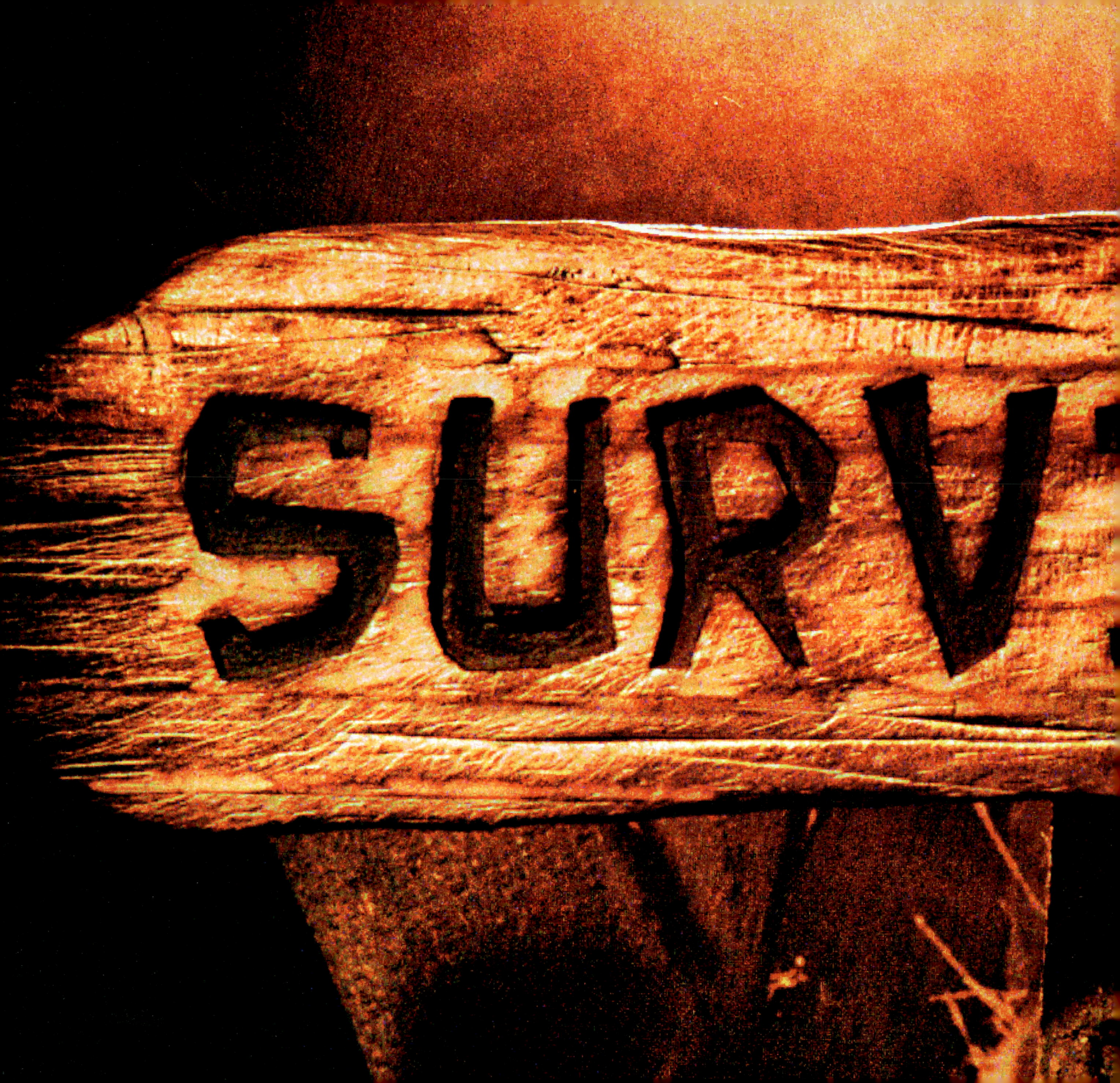
SURV

50 SEASONS

751 PLAYERS

KODAK
8
8
8A